Untitled (Blue Garbo), 13" x 30"

LARRY LEWIS

1919 - 2004

Printed in the United States of America.

ISBN:
978-0-615-51922-7 - Paperback

DISCOVERED MASTERWORKS:
THE EXTRAORDINARY COLLAGES OF LARRY LEWIS

Published by
Laughton & Morielli

This book was conceived, created and edited by
Sharyn Prentiss Laughton & Lina Morielli

This catalogue has been published
in conjunction with the exhibition
Discovered Masterworks: The Extraordinary Collages of Larry Lewis
Silvermine Guild Arts Center
New Canaan, CT
Curated by Jonathan Weinberg
September 25 - November 4, 2011.

Catalogue Essay by Jonathan Weinberg

Photography by Lisa Cuscuna

Graphic Design by SandyGarnett.com

Cover Image
Untitled (Colossal Woman: Woman with Camera)

Back Cover Image
Untitled (Man with the Train)

Last Page Photo Credit
Cynthia Hart Designer

DISCOVERED MASTERWORKS: THE EXTRAORDINARY COLLAGES OF

LARRY LEWIS

Ex libris Laurence R. Lewis, woodblock print on rice paper

Untitled (Woman in Hat), 4" x 9"

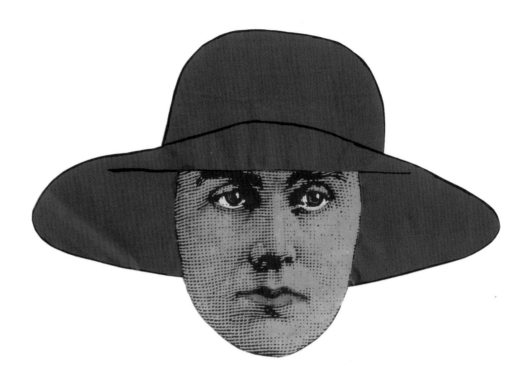

Thank you Larry Lewis for
leaving me your life's work.

Thank you Lina Morielli for your endless knowledge on
all aspects of this project - without you
this journey would never have happened.

Thank you Ben and Ashley
for storing the Larry Lewis art collection -
for being there to help me all the times
I came to work on this enormous project - I love you.

Thank you Tomas for your support, encouragement and listening.

Thank you Jonathan Weinberg for your artistic wisdom and skill -
for your love and appreciation of Larry's art. You have taught me so much -
for this and more I am grateful.

Greta Garbo, 14" x 11"

DISCOVERED MASTERWORKS:
THE EXTRAORDINARY COLLAGES OF LARRY LEWIS
Jonathan Weinberg

Of all the movie stars of the silver screen that Larry Lewis adored or identified with—Fatty Arbuckle, Charlie Chaplin, Joan Crawford, Marlene Dietrich, Lillian Gish, Paula Negri—it was Greta Garbo who cast the strongest spell on the artist. In 1933, just entering his teens, Lewis was so smitten that he made a meticulous copy of her face in her signature role as Queen Christina, the gender-bending monarch who resigns her throne to become a private person. Some forty years later, Lewis was still copying Garbo's movie stills and publicity shots, now by means of the newly invented photocopier machine, tinting and pasting them obsessively into his extraordinary collaged books. In these folios, the Divine Garbo shares the spotlight with less-remembered silent era divas such as Theda Bara, Dorothy Dalton, and Alice Joyce. But while her contemporaries are captured at the height of their beauty and fame, it is only Garbo who ages, captured in retirement by a paparazzo as she wanders the streets of Manhattan on one of her legendary reclusive walks. Her melancholy and restless journeying is juxtaposed with a set of anatomical drawings of eyes, mouths, and ears, as if, despite all of her attempts to hide, she was still the subject of the public gaze and of chattering gossip. We can almost hear her muttering her famous mantra in protest: "I vant to be alone, I vant to be alone..."

Lewis appears to have shared Garbo's desire to live an absolutely private life. Although the mechanisms of celebrity and salesmanship are central to the content of his scrapbooks, Lewis himself did almost nothing to promote himself or his work. He never signed or dated scrapbooks, nor gave them titles. He left no written explanation of their content, and few clues how he imagined they would be exhibited or published. Were it not for the dedicated efforts of the artist Sharyn Prentiss Laughton, his niece-in-law and the executor of his estate, and the help of her loyal friend, the artist Lina Morielli, it might be as though Lewis's art never existed.

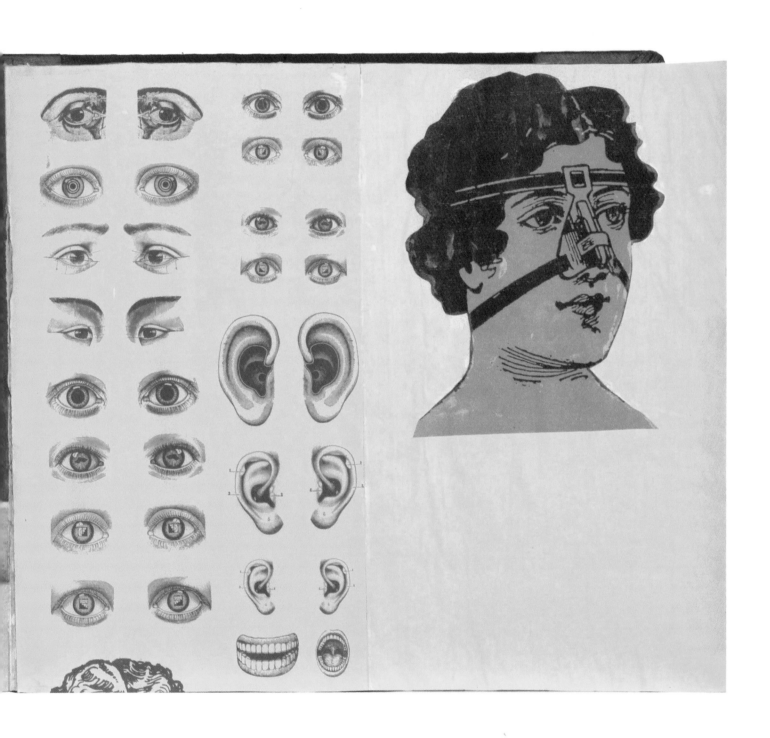

Untitled (Garbo: The Girl and the Game), 13" x 30"

Given Lewis's obscurity, it is perhaps no surprise that Vincent van Gogh was another of his iconic heroes. A magazine article about van Gogh was found pinned to his studio wall at Lewis's death, and van Gogh's image makes several appearances in the scrapbooks. In one memorable spread, Lewis juxtaposes Vincent's face with a Tiffany lamp, an antique cake plate, and a shot of the blond bombshell, Jean Harlow, equating the cult of the Romantic artist with the cult of the movie star, and both with the obsession to collect valuable old things. Did Lewis long for van Gogh's posthumous fame? Perhaps he identified with van Gogh's bouts of depression and loneliness—above all the way in which the very activity of art making for Vincent was a "desperate necessity" that, for a time at least, kept despair at bay.[1] Lewis's fascination with late 19th and early 20th Century advertisements hawking remedies for chronic conditions like constipation or catarrh—a disorder of the nasal passages that was a particular obsession of Lewis's—may allude jokingly to the idea that the artistic temperament was both a disease and a possible form of therapy. We will never know, because Lewis left no body of writings like van Gogh's remarkable letters to explain his work or construct his biography. Despite van Gogh's failure to find success in his lifetime, he was well-known among the Parisian avant-garde, many of whom were friends of his art dealer brother, Theo. In contrast, Lewis, with the exception of becoming a member of the Silvermine Guild—the distinguished artist collective and art school that was near his suburban Connecticut home—was an outsider to the art world. And yet he was not really what is sometimes called an "outsider artist," a term usually reserved for an artist who is self-trained and largely unaware of, or uninterested in, contemporary art and its traditions.

Lewis's Studio (with van Gogh)

Untitled (van Gogh), 13" x 15"

Lewis studied art in school, and as a young man he enjoyed some success as a painter. His elegant still-life paintings of the 1950s show a sophisticated grasp of color and composition. If Lewis seemed uninterested in abstract expressionism, he was nevertheless immersed in the history of modernism, particularly the art of Paul Klee and Giorgio Morandi. Only an artist so steeped in modernism—not only the collages of Max Ernst and Kurt Schwitters, but also the hand-painted cut outs of Henri Matisse, and arguably even the color-field abstractions of Ellsworth Kelly—could be such a master colorist and arranger of shapes as Lewis.

Gouache Paintings 1950's

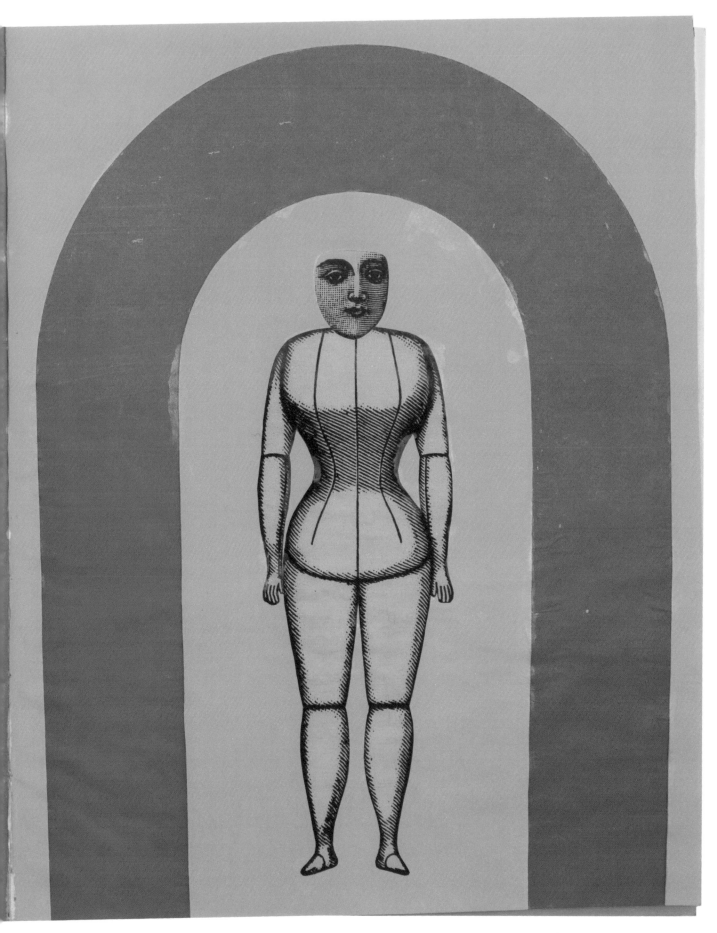

Untitled (Woman With Black Hat), 18" x 29 "

By the 1960s Lewis seems to have largely abandoned traditional easel painting, and his attempt to make a career as a professional artist. He made his living as a secretary for an oil company. Yet, even as he withdrew from the professional art world, he became more fully engaged with contemporary avant-garde trends, particularly Pop art. Although Surrealists like Ernst and Schwitters influenced Lewis's collaging of popular imagery, it was Andy Warhol's equation of the selling of consumer products with the selling of celebrities that provided the crucial example. But, where-

as Warhol idolized the contemporary icons Marilyn Monroe and Liz Taylor, Lewis loved much earlier stars—Garbo, Marlene Dietrich, and Paula Negri. Where Warhol copied Campbell's Soup cans, Lewis preferred tomato products packaged by Balducci's and Pope that had a more traditional, colorful design. The effect was to set the clock back on the roots of Pop, reaching back from the 1950s to a pre-World War II, pre-television generation, almost as if Lewis were self-consciously creating a genealogy of the mass-media that included the period of his own youth.

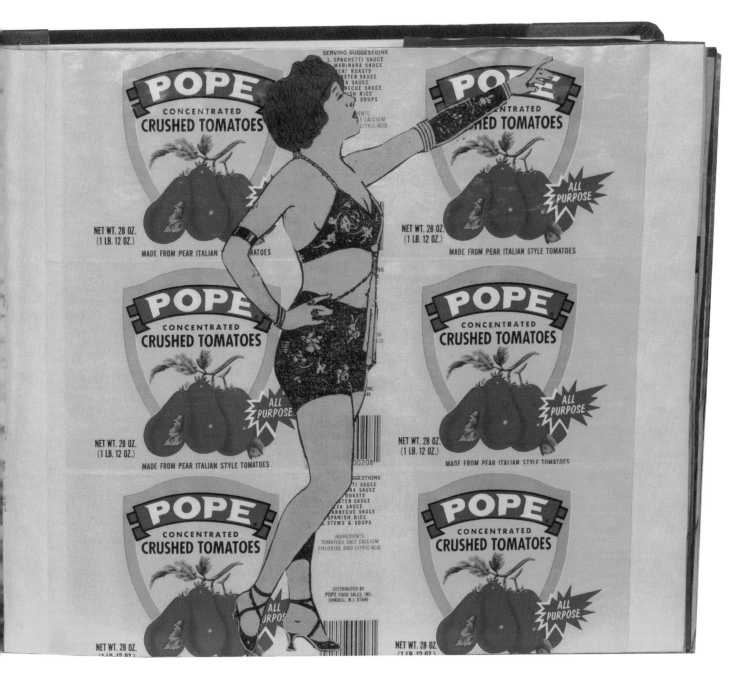

Untitled (Sheltered Daughters), 13" x 30"

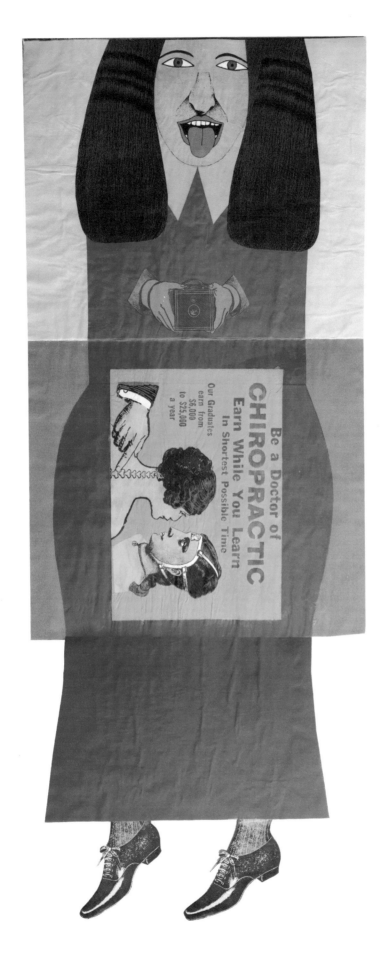

Untitled (Colossal Woman: Woman with Camera), 21" x 53"

Warhol's use of commercial silkscreen techniques, as well as Robert Rauschenberg's method of photo transfers, were important influences on Lewis's use of the photocopier to repeat certain key images in his collage work (the office copy machine became a crucial tool in Lewis's art making in the 1960s soon after his nephew got a job at Xerox). Yet my guess is that Lewis would have been ambivalent about the slick mechanical finish of much of Warhol's work. Significantly, when Lewis invokes Warhol directly by including various pictures of women with nose jobs, the allusion is to one of Warhol's early, so-called hand-painted Pop paintings, *Before and After*, and not one of the more iconic and flat printed silkscreen paintings such as *32 Campbell's Soup Cans* or the *Marilyns*. Like Warhol and other pop artists, Lewis used bright commercial colors in his collages, but differed from Pop practitioners in that his work was clearly hand-brushed. Although Lewis's subject matter was prefigured by Warhol, his sense of painterliness and composition is closer to that of the German-born American artist, Richard Lindner, whose work is sometimes considered proto-Pop. This is particularly true of Lewis's colossal women fold-outs and his brightly colored grotesque female faces. Another possible influence is the collage art of Ray Johnson, which was often based on images from Hollywood films. Whereas Lewis identified with Garbo and Charlie Chaplin, Johnson was more invested with the careers of Buster Keaton, Elvis Presley, and Veronica Lake. [2] Finally, Joseph Cornell's extraordinary boxes were undoubtedly a model for Lewis who acknowledged that influence by pasting an image of a Cornell collage into the back pages of one of the scrapbooks. Cornell pointed the way to an art that, although constructed out of mechanically made objects and reproductions, is painstakingly assembled, crafted, and worked. Lewis's appropriation of the detritus of everyday life, like Cornell's, never seems deadpan or commonplace. Rather than mirroring or critiquing the emptiness and alienation of modern experience in the manner of the Duchampian ready-made, instead it actively transforms the banal into the extraordinary through the imaginative power of the artist's hand and mind.

Untitled (Head: Birth of a Nation), 18" x 14"

Lewis's obsession with late-Victoriana and early Twentieth Century advertising is even less about personal nostalgia than is his use of Hollywood film stills, since many of the advertisements he photocopied must have pre-dated his own childhood. Lewis's collaging of such material relates to a contemporary sea-change in popular taste in which the industrial decorative arts of the previous century were suddenly highly prized. Dover Publications and stores like Shackman Company on Fifth Avenue thrived on the nostalgia craze by creating cheap facsimiles of children books, paper dolls, and other antique toys. Lewis appropriated such images in much the same way that Terry Gilliam did in his animated sequences for the Monty Python series, which undoubtedly Lewis watched on television (Sharyn Laughton reports that Lewis was a great public television fan).[3] Lewis's scrapbooks, aside from their personal significance and symbolism, are also about contemporary trends and a collective past that we all share.

Although he takes as his subject the origins of the mass media in film and print advertising, one

Untitled (Shinola Saddle Shoes), 13" x 30"

of the great paradoxes of Lewis's art is that his scrapbooks resist mass reproduction and viewership. Susan Stewart writes that in the process of scrapbooking, pasted photographs, drawings, newspaper articles, and advertisements "appropriate certain aspects of the book in general. We might note especially the way in which an exterior of little material value envelopes a great 'interior significance,' and the way both souvenir and book transcend their particular contexts." Scrapbooks and other forms of souvenirs, according to Stewart, "deny the book's mode of mechanical reproduction. You cannot make a copy of a scrapbook without being painfully aware that you possess a mere representation of the original." [4] This is particularly true of Lewis's albums, because they are so heavily painted and collaged. Although Lewis's gridded formats and his technique of pressing and gluing down might seem to aspire to an overall flatness, the actual results are highly textured and three-dimensional. The glue and the layers of tinted washes wrinkle the pictures, a process that was often exacerbated by Lewis's decision to insert wax paper between pages, presumably to keep them from sticking as they dried, but which often had unintended effects. The books are themselves objects, not just collections of flattened sheets.

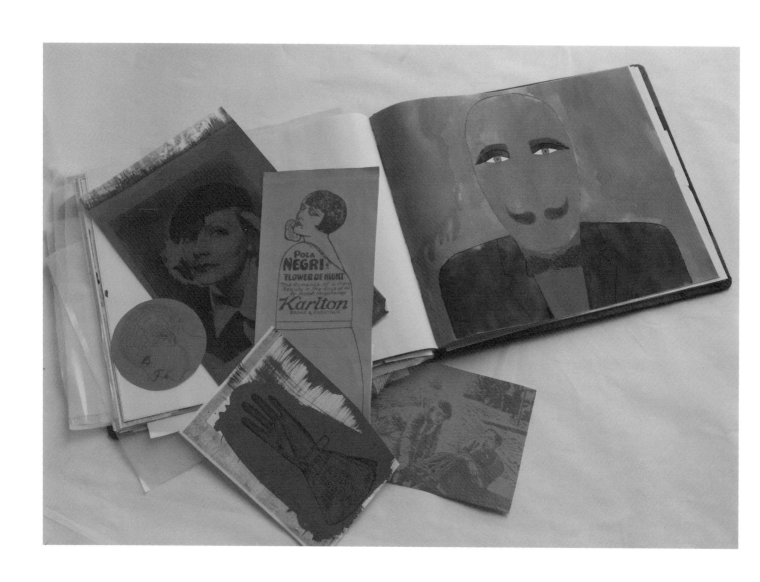

Unfinished Book with Inked Papers

In other ways, Lewis's albums explore the limits of the book form. His first scrapbooks began with store-bought blank folios; later he himself made albums that had a larger vertical format but fewer sheets. His working method can be deduced by examining one of the noticeably unfinished books, in which he had only just begun to paste images. Rather than begin with the first pages and work his way across the album, one spread at a time, he liked to compose several pages simultaneously. He started by dividing certain pages into brightly colored painted rectangles. This process provided the background structure for pasted cutouts. The pictures themselves were usually created by photocopying illustrations and photographs that he found in magazines and books of movie stars, bizarre advertisements, works of art, and strange early modern inventions that caught his fancy. Lewis would often tint the photocopies with highly pigmented inks such as Dr. Martin's, or with glazes of thinned acrylic paint. When he constructed black and white pages, he appears to have heightened the contrast settings of the photocopier, not only to achieve denser blacks but also to make Hollywood divas like Garbo and Bara emerge from a world that is all shadowy darkness. The more he pasted and painted, the thicker the albums became, straining and even breaking their bindings. The books are heavy, so full of pasted pictures, layered glue and they cannot be comfortably read in your hands or even on your lap like a typical picture book. The cutouts themselves sometimes peek out over the edges of the pages, and in some instances, he included elaborate foldout figures whose accordion bodies completely defy the book form's rectangular confines.

Untitled (Ruth Roland & The Star Shirt) 21" x 36"

Untitled (Garbo and Chaplin) 21" x 36"

Untitled (Solid Gold Spectacles) 21" x 18"

Untitled (Alumen Exsic.) 21" x 18"

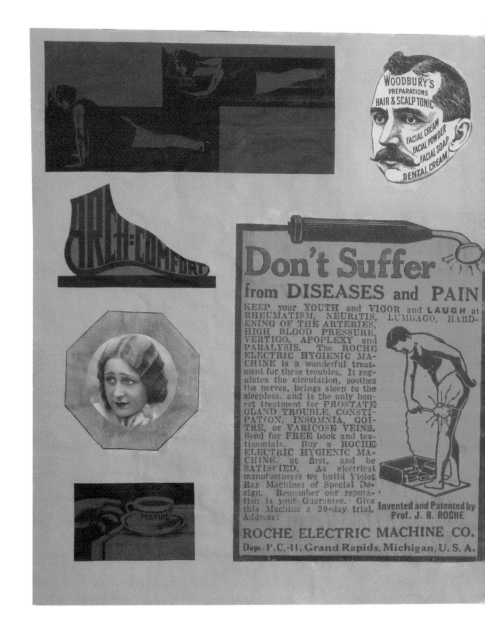

Untitled (Fold Out: Don't Suffer), 21" x 36" (without extension)

If reading these massive books is cumbersome, exhibiting them properly in the traditional spaces of an art gallery is a process of compromise. Choosing to exhibit one spread of any given book means denying the viewer the ability to see all the other spreads. Even when certain damaged books have been taken apart and key images framed, the act of showing one side of a given page inevitably means obscuring its verso. When Lewis made what for him must have been the momentous decision to frame four of the albums in boxes opened to particular spreads, he knew that even in this lone act of exposure he was hiding far more of the work than he was revealing.

Untitled (George Washington Progresso), 13" x 30", framed by Larry Lewis

Untitled (Garbo with MGM Lion), 13" x 15"

Hiding and exposure are fundamental to Lewis's art, I would argue, both formally, in the way that his chosen form both invites and frustrates viewership, and thematically, presenting to us again and again the iconic visage of the seductive but distant movie star. Here Garbo is the ideal type: her face is instantly recognizable, and yet intrinsic to her very allure is her inaccessibility and mystery. Roland Barthes described Garbo as defining "the moment in cinema when capturing the human face still plunged audiences into the deepest ecstasy…when the face represented a kind of absolute state of the flesh, which could neither be reached or renounced." Barthes published his famous discussion of Garbo in his book *Mythologies* which was translated and published in the United States in 1972, at the very time Lewis was collaging his images of Garbo. Barthes, like Lewis, is fascinated by the Garbo of *Queen Christina* in which her face "is almost sexually undefined." Barthes relates her seemingly sculpted features, "at once perfect and ephemeral," to the "flower-white complexion" and "totem-like countenance" of Charlie Chaplin, significantly Lewis's favorite leading man. For Barthes, Garbo's face is divine but also absolutely human. It represents "this fragile moment when the cinema is about to draw an existential from and essential beauty, when the archetype leans towards the fascination of mortal faces, when the clarity of the flesh as essence yields its place to a lyricism of Woman." [5] Visually, Lewis both idolizes Garbo, and suggests her humanity by the contrast of her beauty with the many comic and grotesque faces Lewis painted in the books. These monstrous females are both funny and terrifying. But rather than merely playing contrasting ugly girls to the Hollywood beauty queens, they are more akin to the stars' alter-egos. These Medusas express the misogyny that underlines the cult of the movie star, who is always oscillating between goddess and whore, or as she is sometime described, a siren, a demi-goddess who lures men to their death with her beautiful voice. Whatever her pose and her supposed power, the Hollywood Diva is a construction of her mostly male handlers, the directors, producers and PR men of the patriarchal studio system that assemble and control all the components of her dazzling image. A team of makeup artists and plastic surgeons worked to perfect the body and face of the movie star, augmenting and perfecting her teeth, hair, skin, lips, eye lashes and breasts, in a manner analogous to the construction of Lewis's gigantic fold-out dolls.

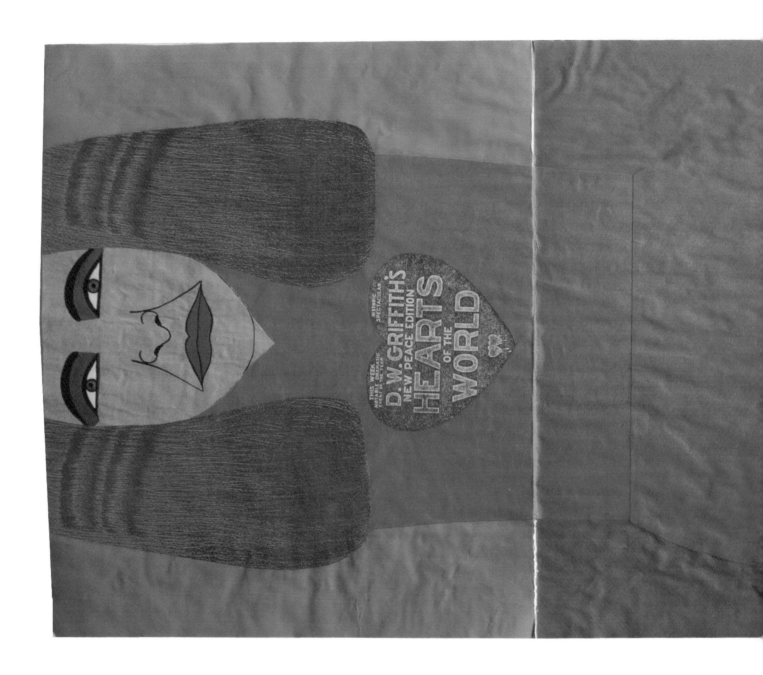

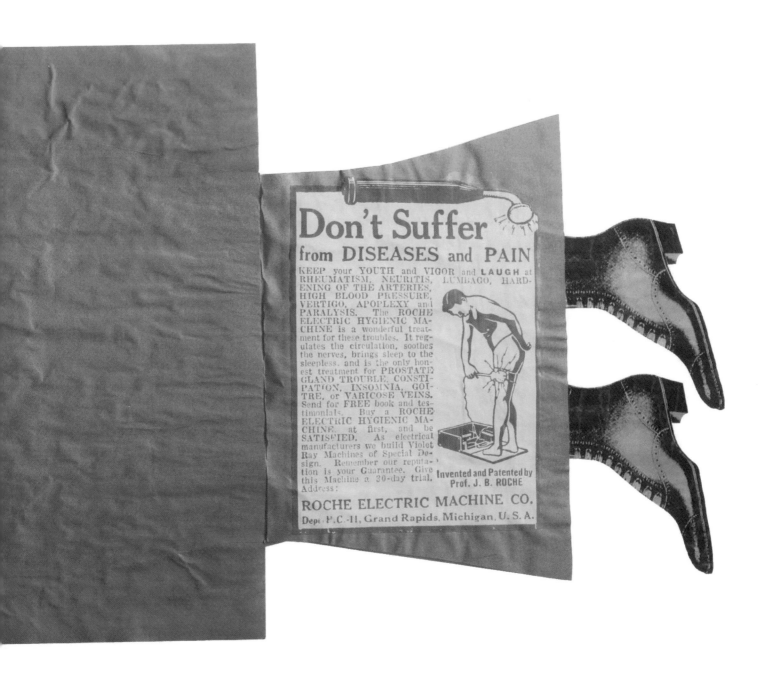

Untitled (Colossal Woman: Hearts of the World), 21" x 53"

And so Lewis's obsession with Hollywood cinema is not just a matter of personal nostalgia. Rather Lewis was taking part in the culture's larger, whole-scale reevaluation of the meaning and significance of American films and the star system, a critique that is still ongoing. While Lewis undoubtedly spent time as a child gazing up at the silver screen, there is something almost generic about the film images he pasted into his scrapbooks that negates the sense that he is trying to recover his lost past. Rather than finding odd moments in films, which might have emphasized the role of his personal memories, he favors the most iconic pictures of divas and comedians. He offers us the Gish sisters in one of the most famous scenes from their career, when they are threatened by a gun in *The Unseen Enemy*, or Theda Bara, vamping as Cleopatra, or the famous paring of Garbo with the Svengalian, Erich von Stroheim in *As You Desire Me*. Clearly, Lewis's work is as much a response to the nostalgia craze of the late-1960s and 70s, when silent pictures were shown in festivals in revival theaters and on public television, as it is a memory project rooted in Lewis's childhood. Lewis's obsession with Fatty Arbuckle suggests, too, that he was well aware of Kenneth Anger's bestselling book, *Hollywood Babylon* (first published in 1959 in French, and later in English in 1965, and reissued and revived many times since) in which Arbuckle is just the most notorious of the many celebrities whose scandalous exploits are recounted in a history that is meant to reveal the perversion and moral hypocrisy of American culture.[6] Although Lewis's scrapbooks don't seem to follow a particular historical narrative in the manner of Anger's book, as a group they cover the entire history of the silent film era in the United States, beginning some seventeen years before Lewis was born with *The Great Train Robbery* of 1902 and encompassing such landmarks as D.W. Griffith's *Birth of the Nation*, Fatty Arbuckle's Keystone Kops movies, and Charlie Chaplin's silent movie career, on into the early talkies. One of the pleasures of looking through the scrapbooks is combining our memory of the wonderful characters the stars played with our knowledge of their often tawdry behavior behind the scene. The supposedly traumatic moment when the gunfighter points and fires his gun at the audience of *The Great Train Robbery*, which Lewis presents repeatedly in the scrapbooks, or the hysterical antics of the Keystone Kops, become associated with the supposedly degraded lives of movie stars, committing real-life murder, suicide, and various other forms of scandalous mayhem that Anger either exaggerated or invented.

Untitled (The Gish Sisters), 13" x 30"

Untitled (The Great Train Robbery), 13" x 30", framed by Larry Lewis

Kenneth Anger was one of the first overtly gay filmmakers and wrote *Hollywood Babylon* in part to validate his own homosexuality, alleging that several famous movie stars like Ramon Novarro and Rudolph Valentino were gay. In a more scholarly vein, Vito Russo and other commentators have focused on the ways in which Hollywood actresses like Garbo and Dietrich frequently played characters that crossed gender boundaries.[7] Garbo in *Queen Christina*, for example, dresses as a young man, fooling the handsome Spanish Ambassador, played by John Gilbert, Garbo's real life lover. Whether because of their supposed private bisexuality, or because of their gender bending roles, an intense identification with Hollywood movie stars has become associated with gay and drag sensibilities, particularly during the period in Ameri-

Untitled (Garbo & Gilbert), 13" x 15"

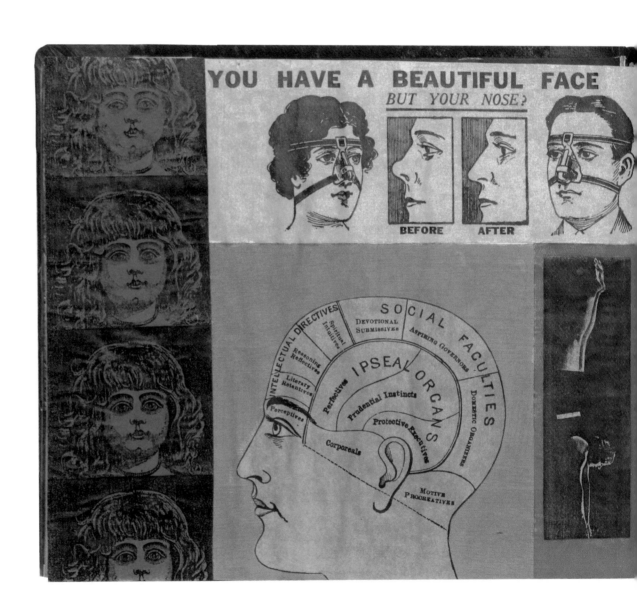

Untitled (You Have a Beautiful Nose), 13" x 30"

can culture when the sketchbooks were being made. But even if Lewis's obsession with movie stars is not necessarily gay in and of itself, when paired with various pictures concerning body dysphoria and the crossing of genders, a potentially queer thematic emerges. Lewis, would probably not have recognized or acknowledged for himself such post-modernist terms, let alone transgender identities, and yet it is remarkable how frequently the appropriated advertising copy touches upon issues of men and women who seem clearly unhappy with the state of the body they were born with. Lewis collected hundreds of late Victorian and early 20th Century advertisements that concerned peculiar diseases of the body which could be cured through the uses of exotic machines, ointments and elixirs. He was also fascinated by prints in which men's and women's bodies are being measured as if for some sort of diet, or studies of different body morphologies. Women and men are captured doing calisthenics, which often doesn't seem to have much effect on their out-of-shape bodies. At the same time, his colossal women have an over-the-top quality that suggests the exaggerated performativity of drag. And many of the large faces of women incorporate photocopied eyes, noses and mouths that appear to come from photographs of men.

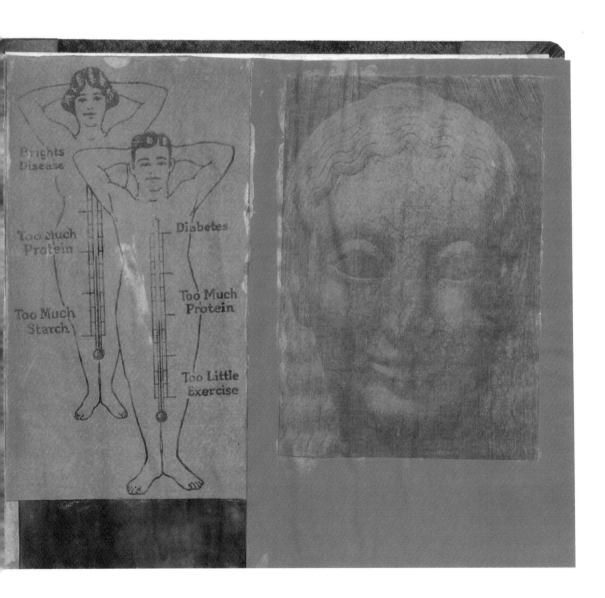

Untitled (Man with the Train), 13" x 30"

For all of their preoccupation with female movie stars, most of the scrapbooks present women's bodies in fragmented ways that undercut their eroticism. Significantly, there is no male equivalent for the monstrous female fold-outs. Yet Lewis does include several beautiful nude men in the scrapbooks, including photographs by Eadweard Muybridge, drawn from his famous studies of the movements of the human body. Rarely does a female character in Lewis's universe seem as unselfconsciously beautiful and natural as Muybridge's athletic youths in the spread Man with the Train. Their confident nudity is in sharp contrast to the mysterious man in the overcoat on the opposing page. His face is cropped above the mouth, creating a sense of anonymity, and he stands by the locomotive as if waiting for a clandestine rendezvous. The juxtapositions of nude and clothed, of purposeful motion and expectant standing in place, create an overall sense of anticipation, longing and unrequited desires.

The word "gay" actually appears on a street sign in one of the only four scrapbooks that Lewis framed himself. The sign says "Nixon's VICTORIA, BALTIMORE ST. NEAR GAY." It is pasted above an image of a young man whose bald head has been marked with various numbered sectors, as if for some sort of phrenological experiment. On either side of this boy are men exercising; above there is a Warholian before-and-after picture of a woman's nose job, as well as a photo of a movie star and a cutout of a pointing finger; to the left area woman in a full-bodied bathing suit and a drawing of an elaborately bandaged foot. On the opposing page, Lewis has painted the garish face of a woman with a big, toothy smile and a yellow hat. Is the phrase "near gay" important, or was Lewis more interested in making a political allusion to the infamous Richard Nixon? Phrenology suggests a method for unlocking the essential character of a subject, but it is this very process that is frustrated by Lewis's cryptic and repetitive use of seemingly disconnected stock images. Nevertheless, what this and so many other Lewis collages evoke is an uneasiness with the bodies we are dealt with, a disconnect between the way we look and the way we feel. Such body dysphoria does not necessarily signal the desire to inhabit a different gender, of course, nor is it necessarily expressive of the condition of the closet in which men and women are forced to hide their sexual identity. After all, central to the kind of advertising imagery and film icons Lewis was obsessed with is the idea that no one who makes up the viewership for the mass media is perfect—everyone can be improved. Not even the movie stars themselves could live up to the ideal of beauty they projected on the silver screen.

Untitled (Nixon's Victoria), 13" x 30", framed by Larry Lewis

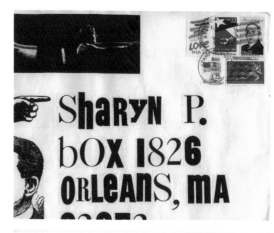

It is always perilous to read an artist's identity through his work; how much more so when, in the case of Larry Lewis, we know so little about his biography and thoughts other than that he lead a conventional married life with his wife, Bebe Nemeth. In the end, the most personally revealing aspect of the scrapbooks is not their possible symbolism or narrative content, but rather the restless obsessiveness of their imagery. It is as if Lewis were reworking the same ideas and feelings over and over again. Laughton reports that Lewis felt that he never was finished working on any of the scrapbooks.[8] He was always starting new books before the old books were completed, although he would keep returning to the older volumes to add new layers of images. He continued to repeat many of the same motifs and compositions, as if they were all part of some larger, multi-volume corpus. This failure to bring a book to completion is one with Lewis's reluctance to arrange for their exhibition. My guess is that the actual process of making the books was so important to his sense of being that to finish and exhibit them would have been a kind of death. If this is true, how deep must have been Lewis's faith in Sharyn Laughton? Laughton's own modest and loving memoir of Lewis, published in this volume, hints at the qualities of charm, wisdom and tact that so endeared her to him. He came to trust her so much that he did not simply make a bequest of his life's work to her, knowing she would care for it - he even went so far as to initiate her into the alchemy of his art-making before he died, sending her elaborately decorated envelopes that enclosed cut-out pictures for her to collage herself. These were accompanied by a few words of instructions:

This is a sample lot of material for anybody who would like to try out my collage book technique. Have a go and see what happens. Perhaps you would prefer to use your own materials instead!
XXXX Larry

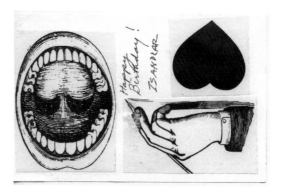

Let us take these brief words of the artist, so rarely offered in Lewis's case, as his testament for us all, enjoining us to make of his marvelous collages what we will for our own psychic well-being. The result will be that we have kept his marvelous art alive, rescuing it from obscurity.

Larry with Framed Collage Book

Lewis mail sent to Sharyn

Untitled (Benett Hairpins) 13"x 15"
Untitled (Girl with Black Hair) 13" x 15"
Untitled (Mia) 13" x 15"

Untitled (Garbo with Dolls) 13" x 15"
Untitled (Man with Black Hat) 13" x 15"
Untitled (An Eye Opener) 13" x 15"

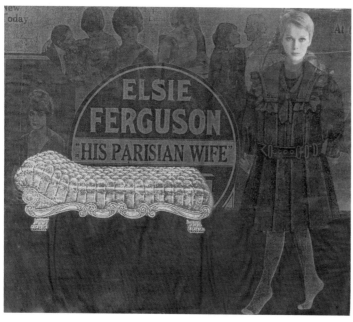

Untitled (Head: Woman with Blue Eye Shadow), 13" x 15"

Untitled (Head: Woman with Red Hair), 18" x 14"

Untitled (Boy with Bubble Pipe - Blue), 13" x 15"

Untitled (Woman with Green Chaise Longue), 13 " x 15"

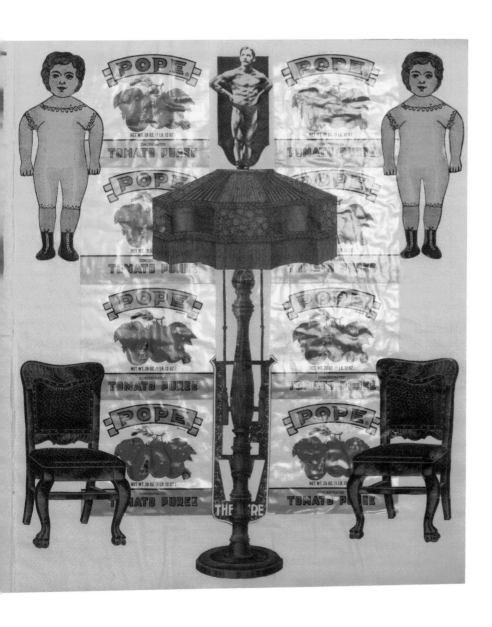

Untitled (Fold Out: Pope Tomatoes), 21" x 36" (without extension)

Untitled
(Garbo & Von Stroheim)
13" x 30"

Untitled
(Victorian Father & Child)
13" x 30"

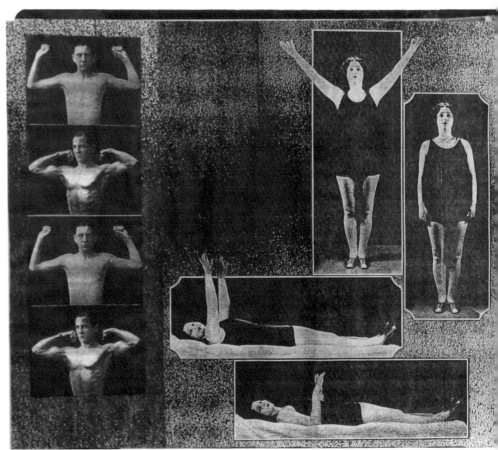

Untitled
(Send No Money)
13" x 30"

Untitled
(Pola Negri)
13" x 30"

Untitled (Colossal Woman: Why Girls Leave Home?), 21" x 53"

My Memories of Larry Lewis

Sharyn Prentiss Laughton

I met Larry Lewis in the late 1960's. We both had married into a very close Hungarian family. Larry was married to Bebe Nemeth and my mother-in-law was Mimi Prentiss, Bebe's sister. Family and art drew us together; Larry supposing I knew something about art having just graduated from college with a BFA and me being excited to relate to an artist in my new family.

Larry worked as a secretary at United Oil Products. His art studio was in his home. He drove a red car and lived in a red house. He collected cobalt blue glass objects and in the summer he had a multitude of green plants in red clay pots. He transported home cooked food from sister to sister; sister to brother and family to family......it was a full time job.

Larry's early art, which were oil paintings, hung on the walls where I lived. In the late 60's he had begun creating incredible art books. He called them collage books. He was completely enthralled with the possibilities that photocopying offered. His nephew, who worked at Xerox, photocopied the images from old publications that Larry would then use for his collages. He would apply bright colored inks to the reproductions and then add his own hand. I was fascinated by his art as we turned the pages of his collage books in his studio. No book was ever completely finished, but that didn't stop him from beginning a new one.

I was fortunate that Larry shared his art with me because Larry shared his art with very few, if any. He had no ambition of being acknowledged and no interest in selling his art. Larry had very little desire for an exhibition either. I believe his passion was in the journey, the process. I often shared with him my visual dream of walking into a gallery filled with his books placed in glass cases with pages being turned electronically.

After I moved from Connecticut to Cape Cod, Larry and I began to correspond by mail. He sent me decorated envelopes containing his photocopied images with instructions for use or to give away. We saw each other on his annual summer visits to Truro and Provincetown and then when I would visit him in Connecticut. Art was our mutual connection, attraction and was the basis for our friendship.

As the years passed and Larry's health declined, our encounters were few. My last memory is of visiting Larry in the hospital with a bouquet of sunflowers which signified our mutual love for van Gogh.

Why didn't I ask him questions about his art?

Larry left me the contents of his red house. He left me his art; the entire collection of his life's work. Why?

I was in California caring for my Mom when I was contacted and informed that Larry's home was recently sold and the contents had to be removed quickly.

Who would complete this daunting task?

I called my friend and artist Lina Morielli. Lina lived in Stamford, CT. near Larry's red house in Rowayton. Lina, who had never met Larry or seen his art, said yes.

Lina cataloged, organized, labeled, discovered, identified, appreciated, went crazy, disassem-

bled Larry's studio and packed it up. Lina loved Larry's art as much as I did and marveled at his extraordinary sense of color, composition and style.

We thought, this is good – this is very good.

We began the journey together – exploring the endless possibilities of showing the masterworks of Larry Lewis's extraordinary collages.

We met Jonathan Weinberg a curator, educator, art historian, and artist.

We met Jeffrey Mueller – Gallery Director of Silvermine Guild Arts Center.

Larry Lewis…………..we have begun.

My Introduction to Larry Lewis

Lina Morielli

I walked into Larry Lewis's house to begin the chore I had been asked to do; dispose of his personal effects and look at his art work.

The house looked like any other that had not been lived in for a while. The air was still and a thin layer of dust coated everything. The house was dark, dreary and conspicuously colorless but neat and orderly. The furnishings were sparse and tired looking but functional. You could not tell from the furnishings who had lived there. I found his studio (a converted porch) on the far side of the living room. The contrast between the house and the studio was like night and day. The walls were covered with everything from newspaper clippings, photos of van Gogh, giant sized, brightly colored paper cutouts of women and other ephemera. It was like a giant bulletin board. Piles of old ledger notebooks were stacked on the floor. These were the books that Sharyn had told me to look at. I opened one and the color jumped right off the page. The images went from bizarre collages of pieced together women's faces to photocopied and painted Victorian newspaper ads. Each page looked like a painting unto itself. I slowly looked around this studio. There were bookcases and standing files filled with brightly colored inked sheets of paper and boxes of photocopied images and I mean hundreds of images. He used Dr. Martin's Inks and acrylic paints, mediums, Elmer's Glue and his paint brushes were the size of house painting brushes and each one was stained in a brilliant color. There was another pile of books that were hand built with black and white covers filled with images of everything from movie stars of the 20's and 30's to apothecary bottles and ads for potions all glued to brilliant neon pink and acid green grounds. I found old paintings done in the 1940's and some drawings from middle school. As I began to organize furniture and other personal objects for donation or disposal I found more collage books tucked inside kitchen cabinets and the nightstand by his bed. I went to the cellar and there was a bookcase on the back wall filled with magazines from the 1920's that were so moldy they fell apart in my hands. I found art work everywhere. Folders full of old newspaper ads dating back 50 and 60 years, a dozen pieces of framed art shoved under stacks of boxes. I opened up an old book and found a wood cut print and then another and also one from a local artist named Harry Townsend and one from Ross Abrams. It was never ending.

I took snapshots of the studio and took a few notebooks home to show people in the art community and everything else went into storage. I felt very strongly about the work but even more interested in Larry. Who was this man who never or rarely ever exhibited his work? Almost nothing was signed or dated and nothing was archived. He was just leaving it behind to Sharyn as if to say, "Do what you will."

It does my heart good to know that Larry's work will be presented at last and I feel fortunate that I have been involved in the process of bringing his art to the public.

Art in any stage of development is important because it reflects the time in which artists live and is as important to the fabric of community as any business or institution. It can be beneficial when artists take the extra step to archive their work and make plans for it after they are gone. The art, whether visual, performed, written or filmed, created individually or as a collective, must be valued and considered a contribution to the cultural growth and well being of the community.

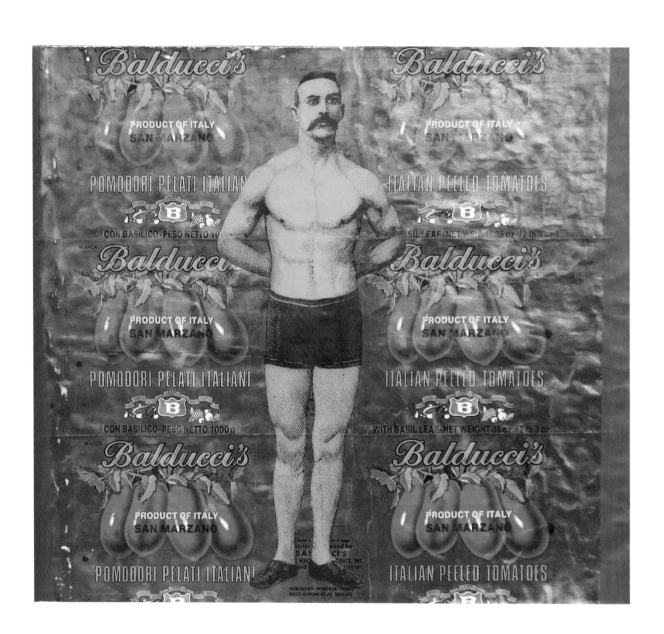

Untitled (Balducci's), 13" x 15"

Jonathan Weinberg Bibliography and Essay Notes

Jonathan Weinberg (Ph.D. Harvard 1990) is a painter and art historian. He is the author of *Male Desire: the Homoerotic in American Art (2005); Ambition and Love in Modern American Art (2001);* and *Speaking for Vice: Homosexuality in the Art of Charles Demuth, Marsden Hartley and the First-American Avant-Garde (1993).* He is a Visiting Critic at the Yale University Art School and a Lecturer at the Rhode Island School of Design. He was a recipient of a 2002 Guggenheim Fellowship and a 2009 grant from the Creative Capital/Andy Warhol Foundation. A one-man retrospective of his paintings was on view at the Leslie Lohman Foundation in New York in 2010. Along with Barbara Buhler Lynes, he co-curated the 2011 exhibition *Shared Intelligence: American Painting and the Photograph* as well as co-edited the catalogue for the Georgia O'Keeffe Museum.

Essay Notes

I would like to thank my partner Nicholas Boshnack and my friend, Joseph Fouse for their advice on this essay.

[1] For a discussion of the role art might play in the ego formation of the artist see Eugene David Glynn, *Desperate Necessity: Writings on Art and Psychoanalysis*, 1st ed. (Pittsburgh, PA: Periscope Pub., 2008).

[2] Ray Johnson's work in the 1970s was not as well known as Cornell, Warhol or Lindner, however, an indicator that Lewis was aware of Johnson's art, at least at the end of his life, is the collaged letter that Lewis sent Sharyn Laughton that I briefly discuss at the end of this essay. Johnson is considered the father of this kind of mail art. For a discussion of Ray Johnson's art and its relationship to many of the same themes I discuss in Lewis's work see Jonathan Weinberg,"Ray Johnson Fan Club," in *Ray Johnson: Correspondences*, ed. Donna Desalvo (New York: Flammarion, 1999), 95-109.

[3] Sharyn Prentiss Laughton interview with the author.

[4] Susan Stewart, *On Longing: Narratives of the Miniature, the Gigantic, the Souvenir*, the Collection, 1st paperback ed. (Durham: Duke University Press, 1993), 139.

[5] Roland Barthes, *Mythologies*, trans. Annette Lavers (New York: The Noonday Press, 1972), 59.

[6] Kenneth Anger, *Hollywood Babylon* (New York: Dell Publishing, 1975).

[7] Vito Russo, *The Celluloid Closet: Homosexuality in the Movies* (New York: Harper, 1981).

[8] Sharyn Prentiss Laughton interview with the author.

Polaroid by Cynthia Hart

Sharyn and Lina in the mid 1980's the day they met

Cynthia Hart's Studio 902 Broadway NYC

CPSIA information can be obtained
at www.ICGtesting.com
Printed in the USA
253710LV00005BA